Music - Home of Middle C

and

Songs - Featuring Middle C

By Mary Anne Miceli

Artwork by Dianne Gagnon Caputo

Music - Home of Middle C
and
Songs - Featuring Middle C

Copyright © 2015

ISBN: 978-0-9888654-4-0

This a work of fiction. Names, characters, places,
and incidents either are the product of the author's
imagination or are used fictitiously, and any
resemblance to any actual persons, living or dead,
events, or locals is entirely coincidental.

All rights reserved. No part of this book may be reproduced or transmitted in
any form or by any means, electronic or mechanical including photocopying,
recording, or by any information storage and retrieval system, without
permission in writing from the copyright owner.

This book is written, published and copyrighted by Mary Anne Miceli.

This book is printed and published in the
United States of America.

ABOUT THE AUTHOR

Mary Anne is a Boston native of Irish extraction and has studied her Irish ancestral roots. Mary Anne has always loved nursery rhymes and music. She so likes the beat of 'rhythm and rhyme', she thinks and composes in 'rhyming rhythm'. Mary Anne feels that life itself has 'rhythmic processes' of highs and lows like the ebb and flow of the tides.

She feels writing is the hallmark of the creative process as it 'purges the soul and inspires the mind.'

Mary Anne lives in a picturesque town on the North Shore of Boston and continues to write both Children's Picture Books and Poetry.

Her published books: *Boston North Shore's Rhyming Fish Tales; Boston North Shore's Salem's Golden Broomstick; Boston North Shore's Teeny, Tiny, Ticks; Boston North Shore's Mouse Tales of Early Salem; Boston North Shore's Tales of Webs; Boston North Shore's Car Wash Squid; China Baby Doll; How 'Pilly - Pine', the Alpaca, Lost his Quills; Confessor's Animal Wartime Blues; Poetry: Reflecting on the Clouds of Everyday Living; Poetry: Aging Ever So Gracefully; Poetry: Everyday Musings; and Poetry: Death Chimes.*

Introduction

Music is the universal language and combines sound, rhythm and melody to delight, comfort and soothe listeners of all ages.

The Piano is the major instrument for musical expression, and Middle C, the middle note of the piano, is the beginning note of the C Scale and C Chord.

This book introduces youngsters to the piano in an artistic way by personifying the note, Middle C, in a playful and magical way.

Music - Home of Middle C

and

Songs - Featuring Middle C

I'd like to introduce you to my home
Where music notes musically roam

I am Middle C, known as 'Do', (pronounced 'doe')
Other notes follow me, up and down, in rows

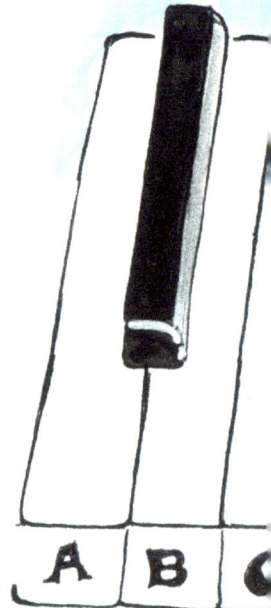

For, I am the beginning note of the musical scale
And, the middle note of the piano's <u>musical</u> rail

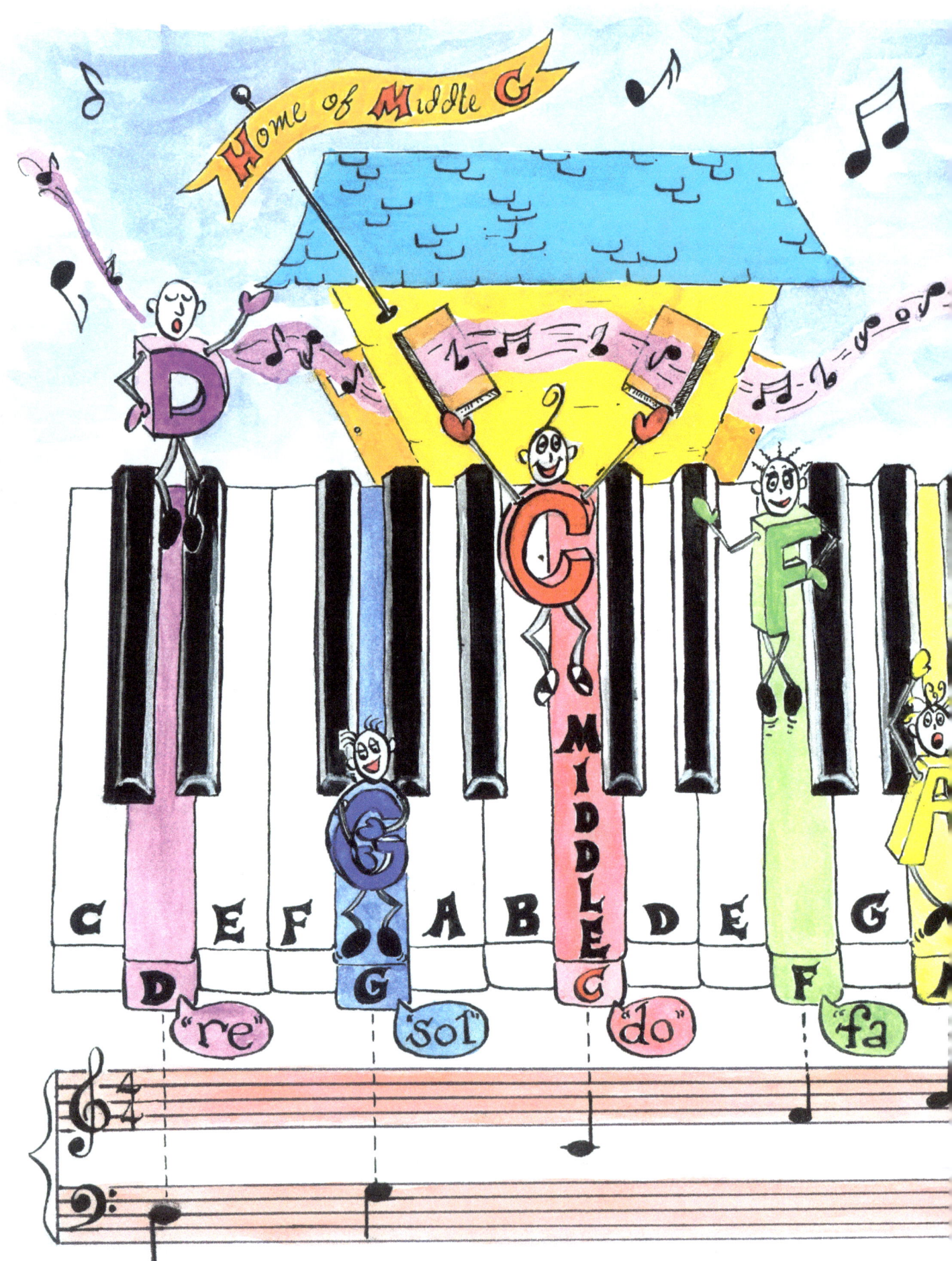

I live in the middle of my piano home
Where musical sounds freely roam

As many piano notes can be played at one time
Producing well-known rhythms and rhymes

Our note sounds can easily mingle
Into any number of songs and jingles

Home of middle C
C D E F G A B C D E F G A B C D
Left Thumb

C D E F

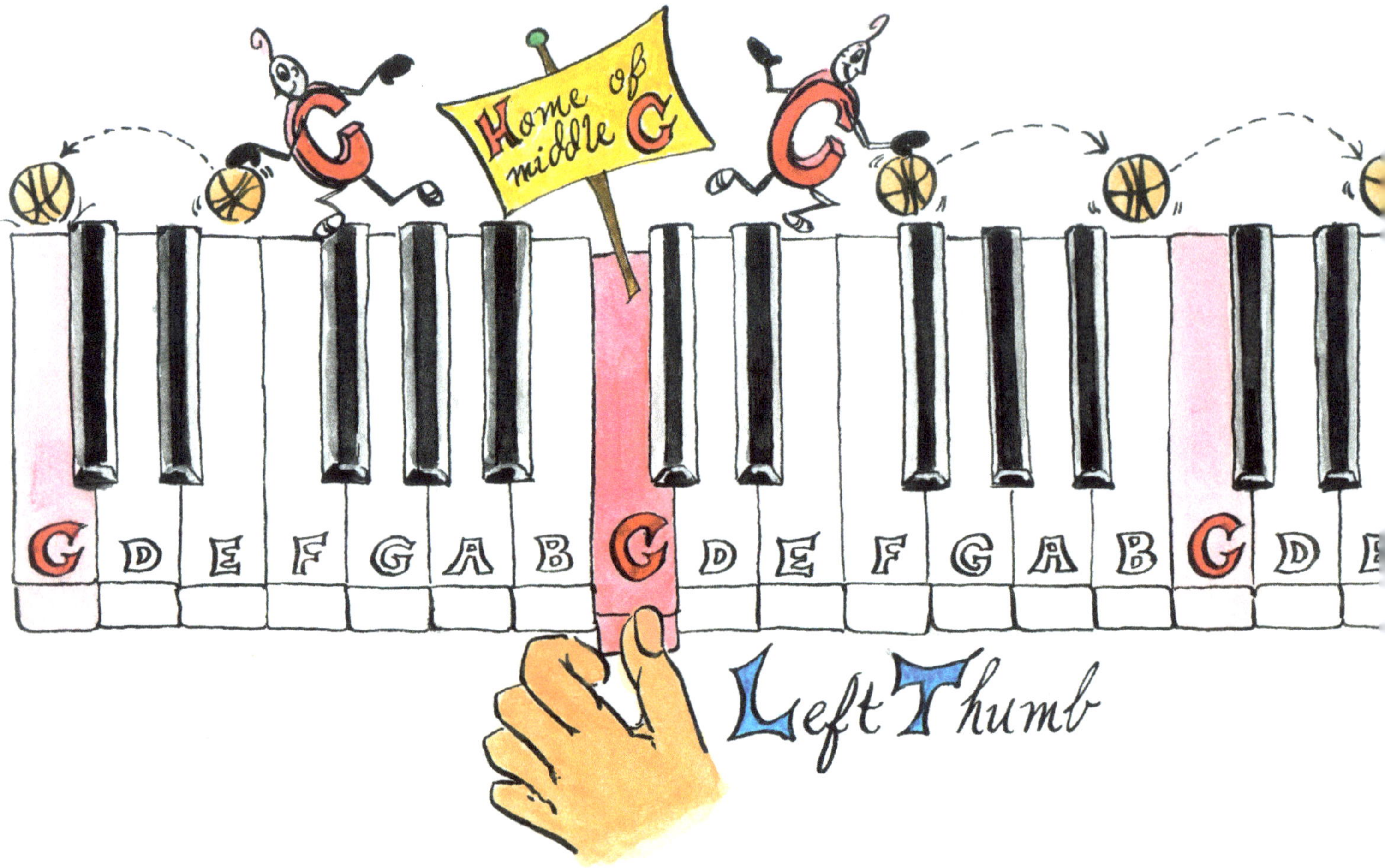

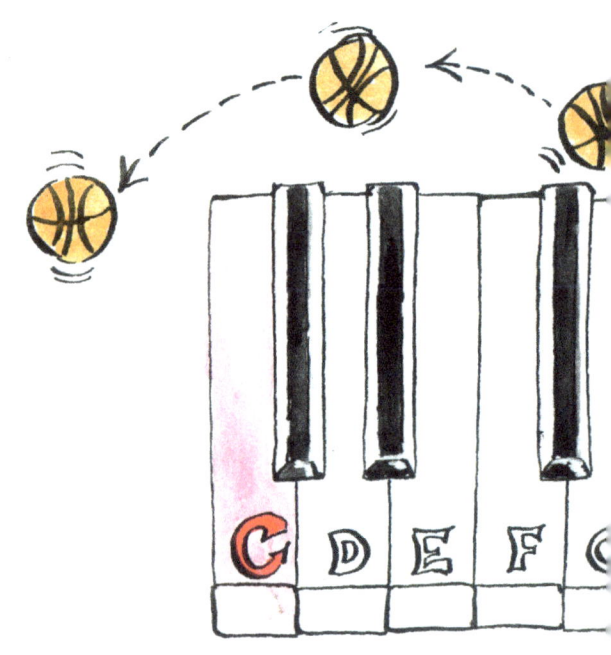

F
G
A
B
C

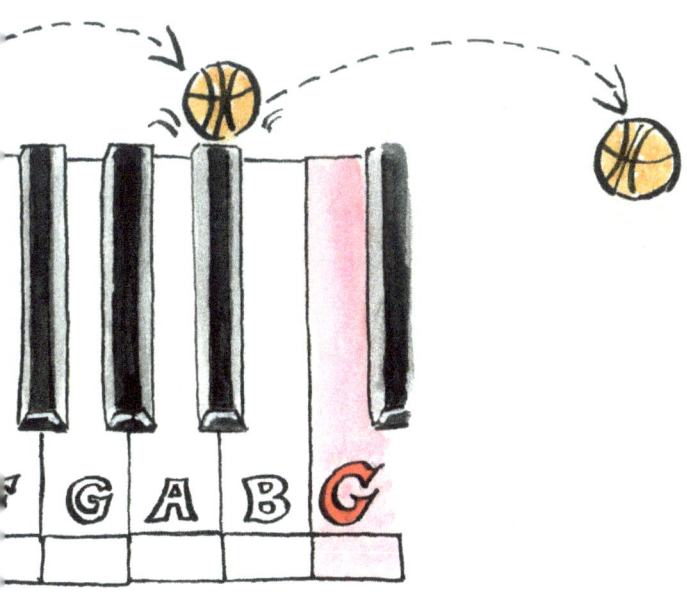

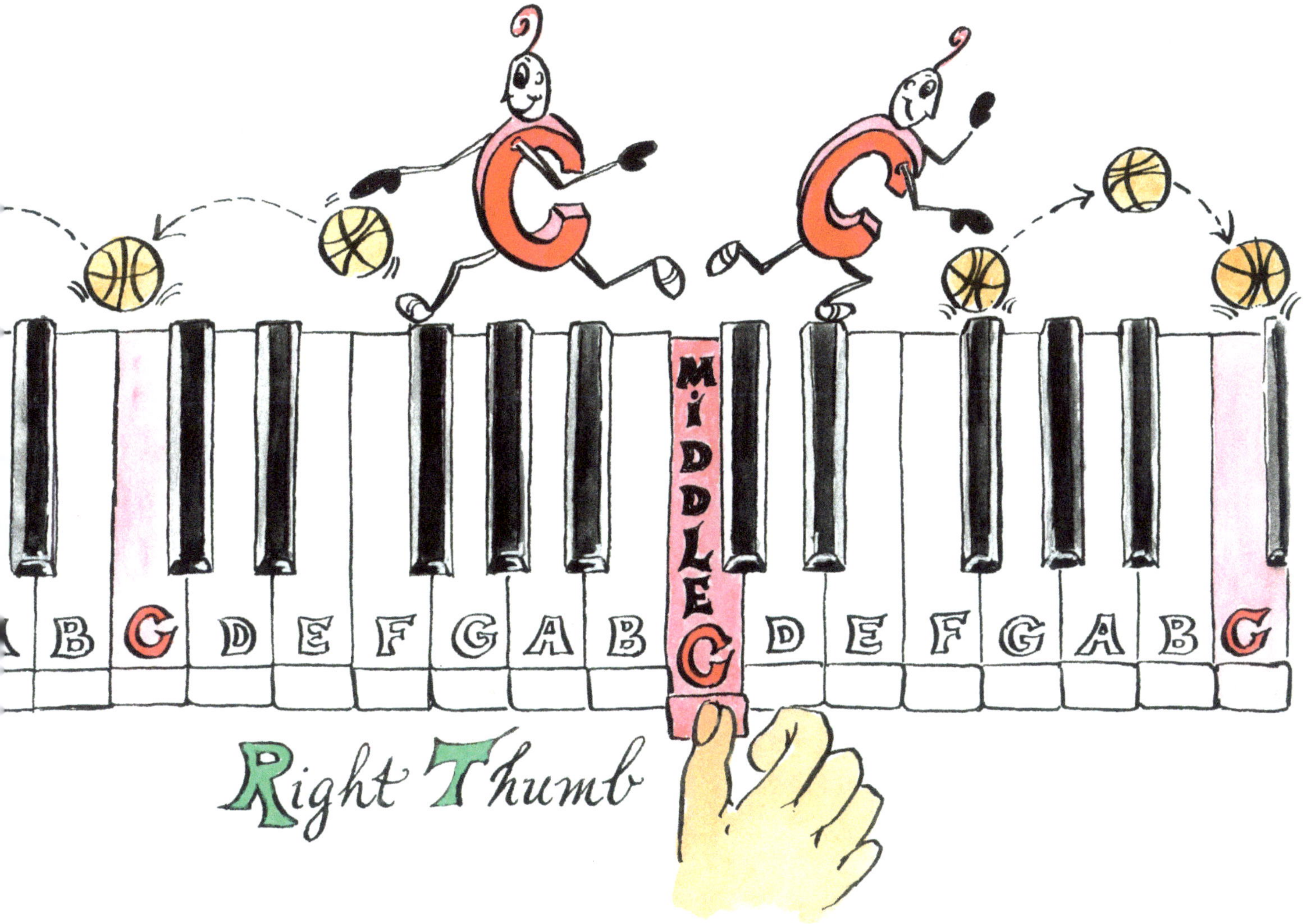
A
B
C
D
E
F
G
A
B
MIDDLE C
D
E
F
G
A
B
C
Right Thumb

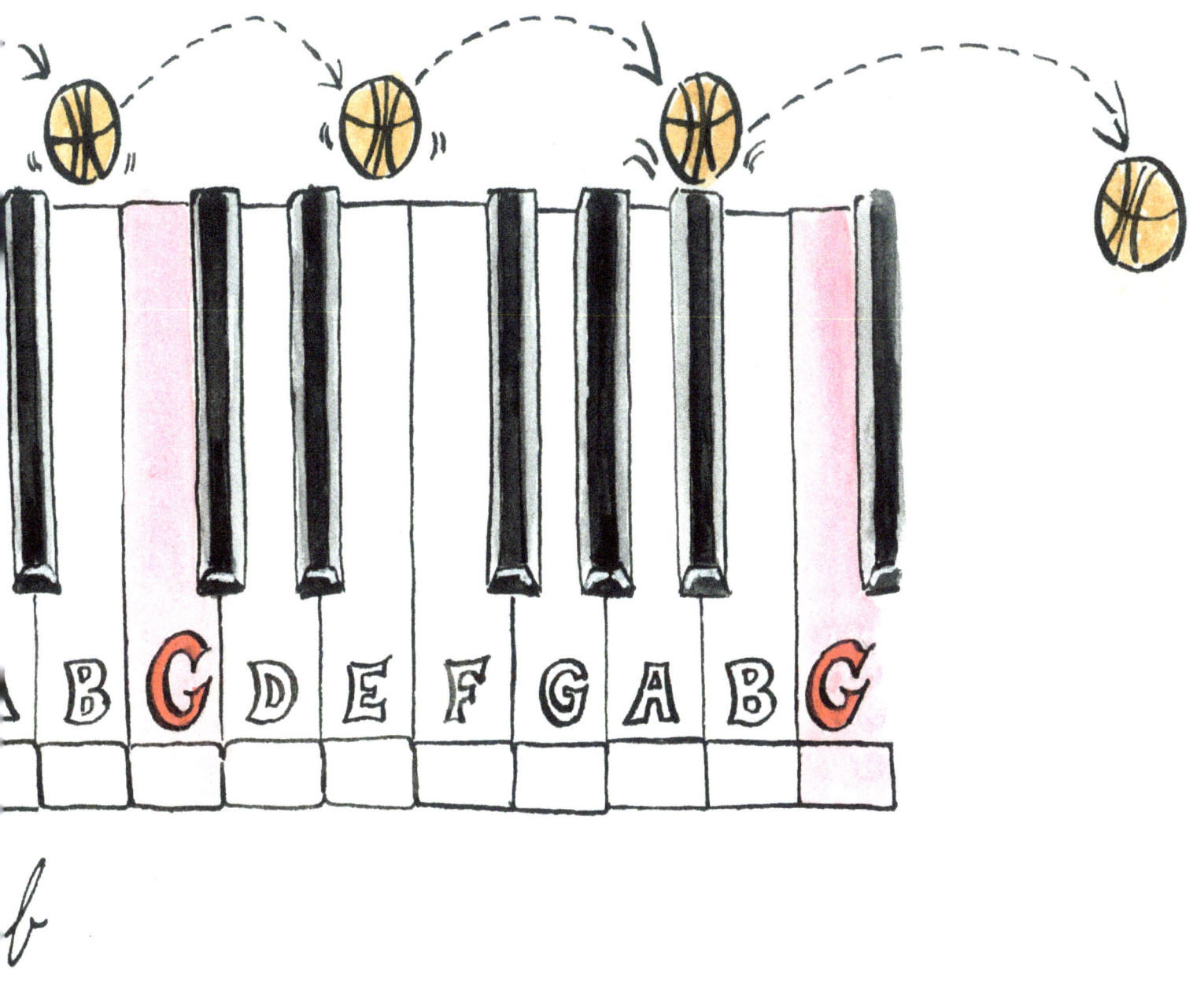

Find me in the piano's middle place
Touch the key and note the space

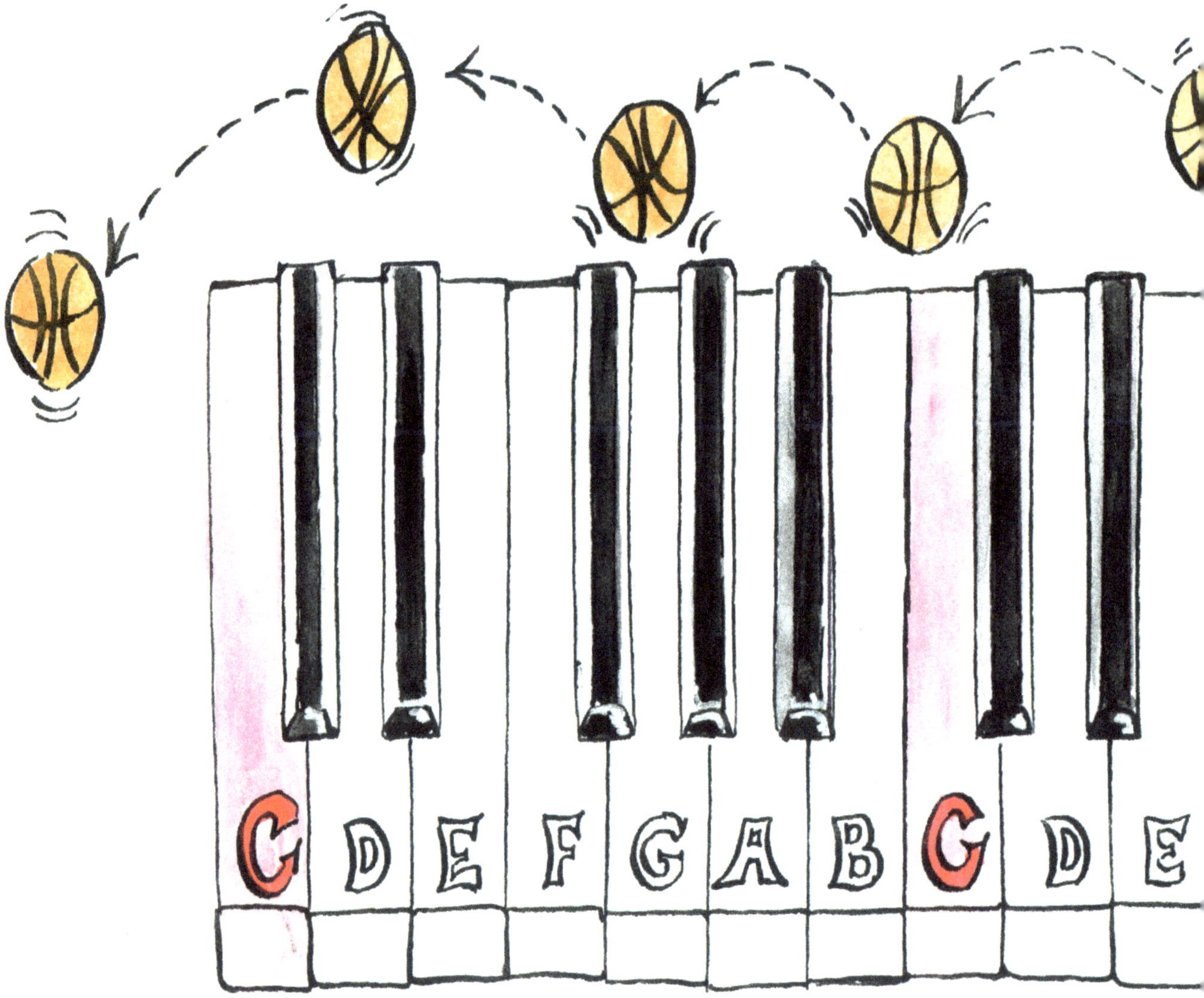

Dribble the scales with your finger tips
Beginning at Middle C with your right thumb tip
Up the scale you will climb
From Middle C up to the next C in line
An octave up, a higher C
Then dribble back down to Middle C

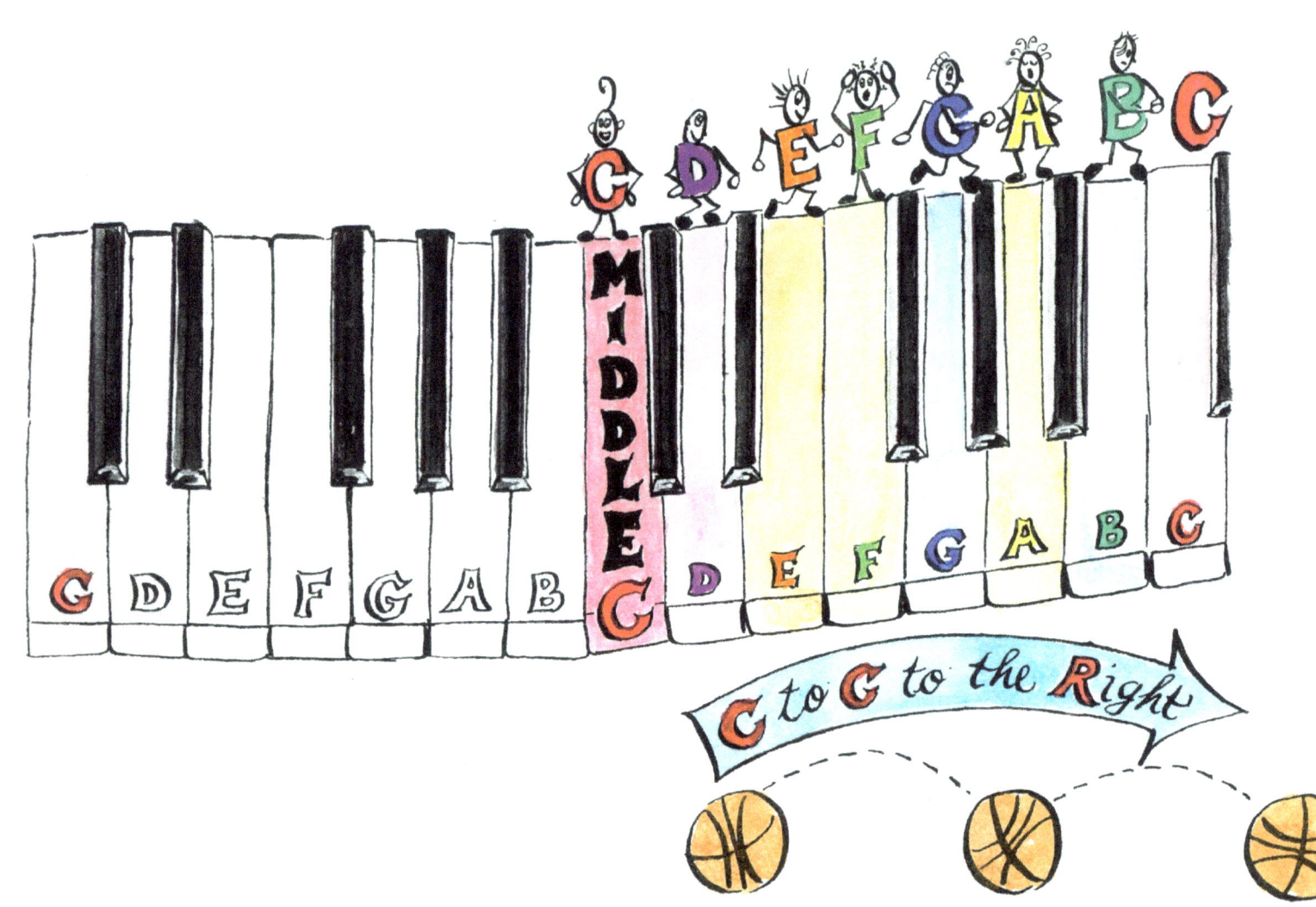

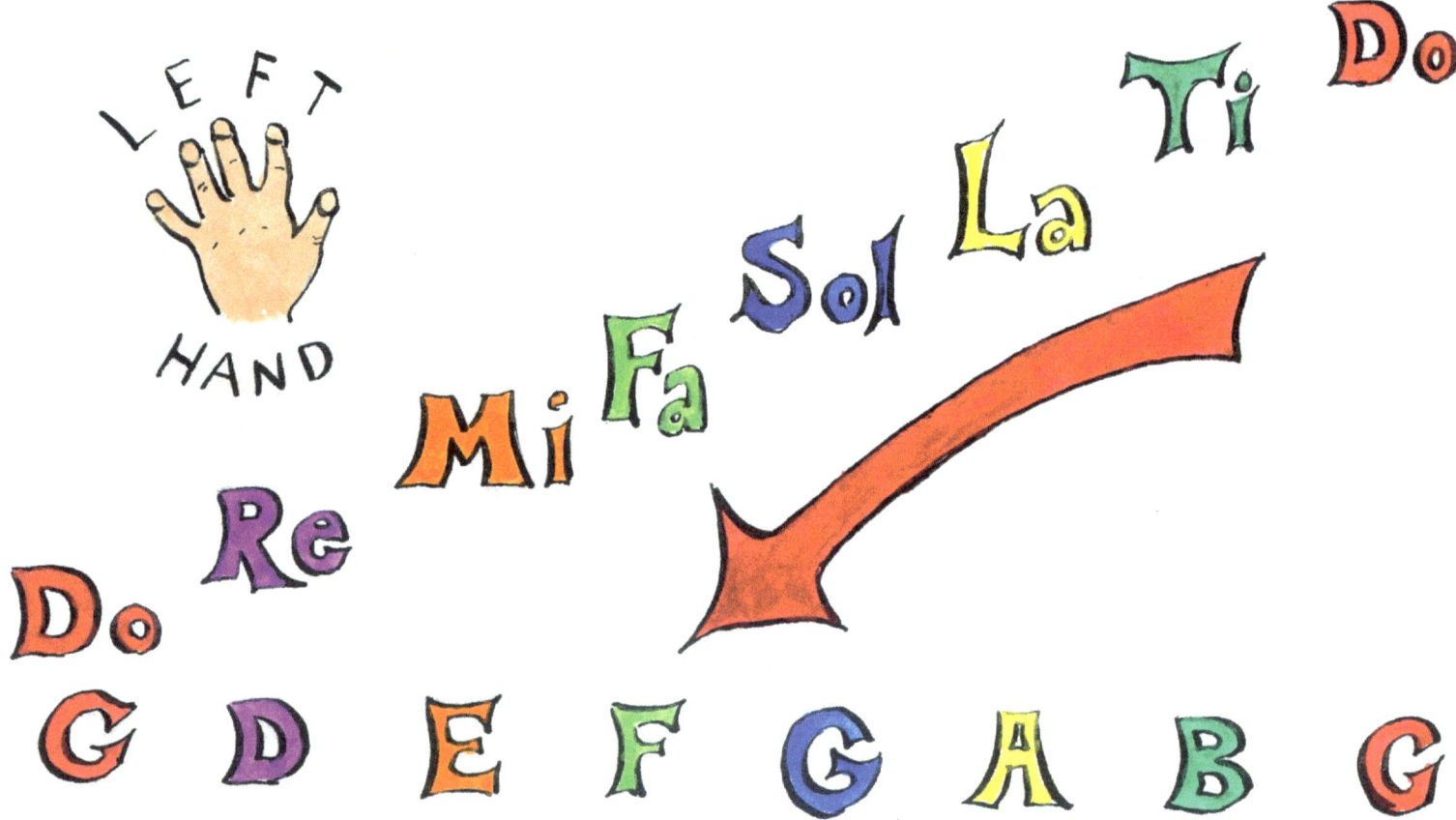

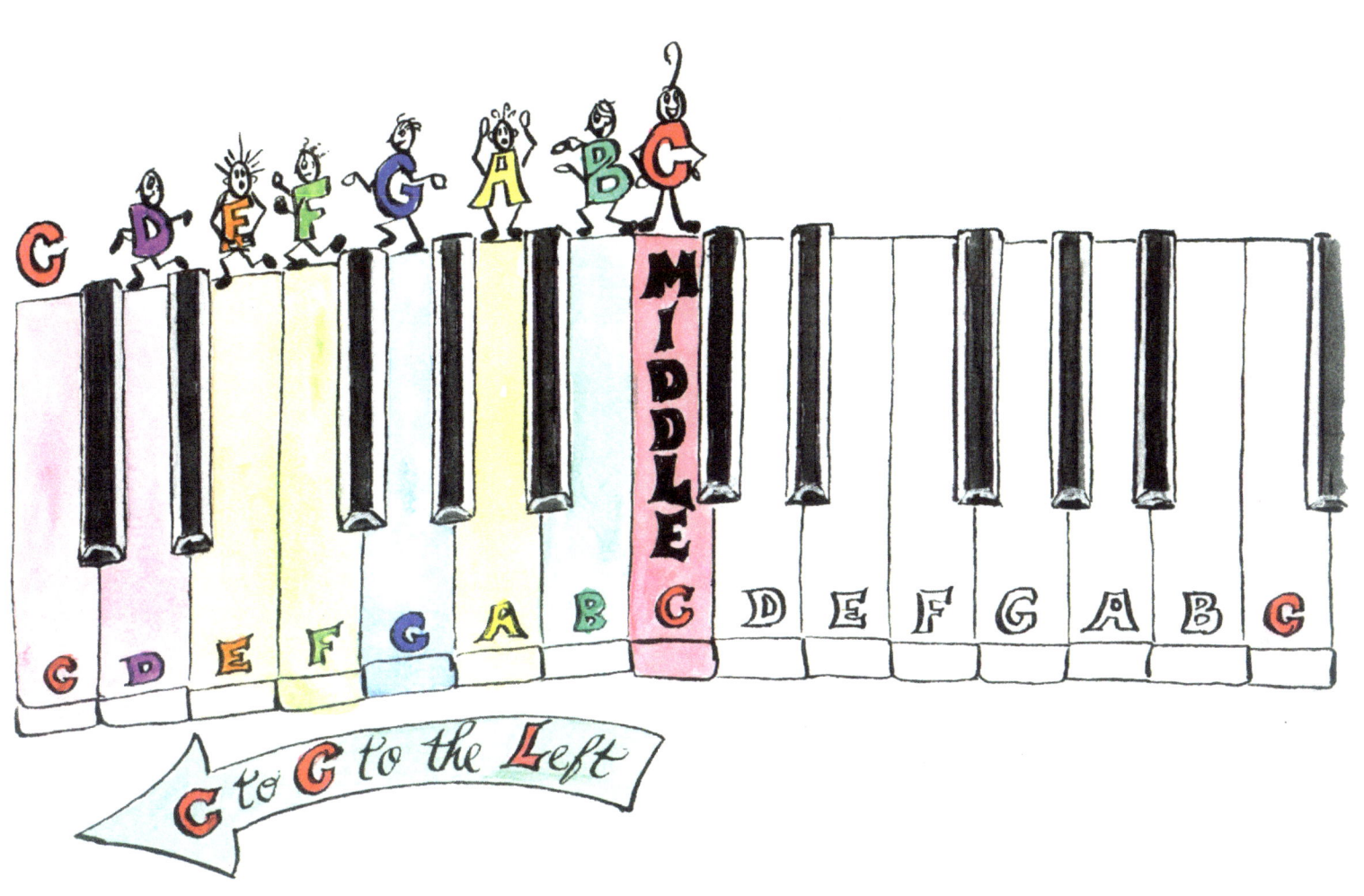

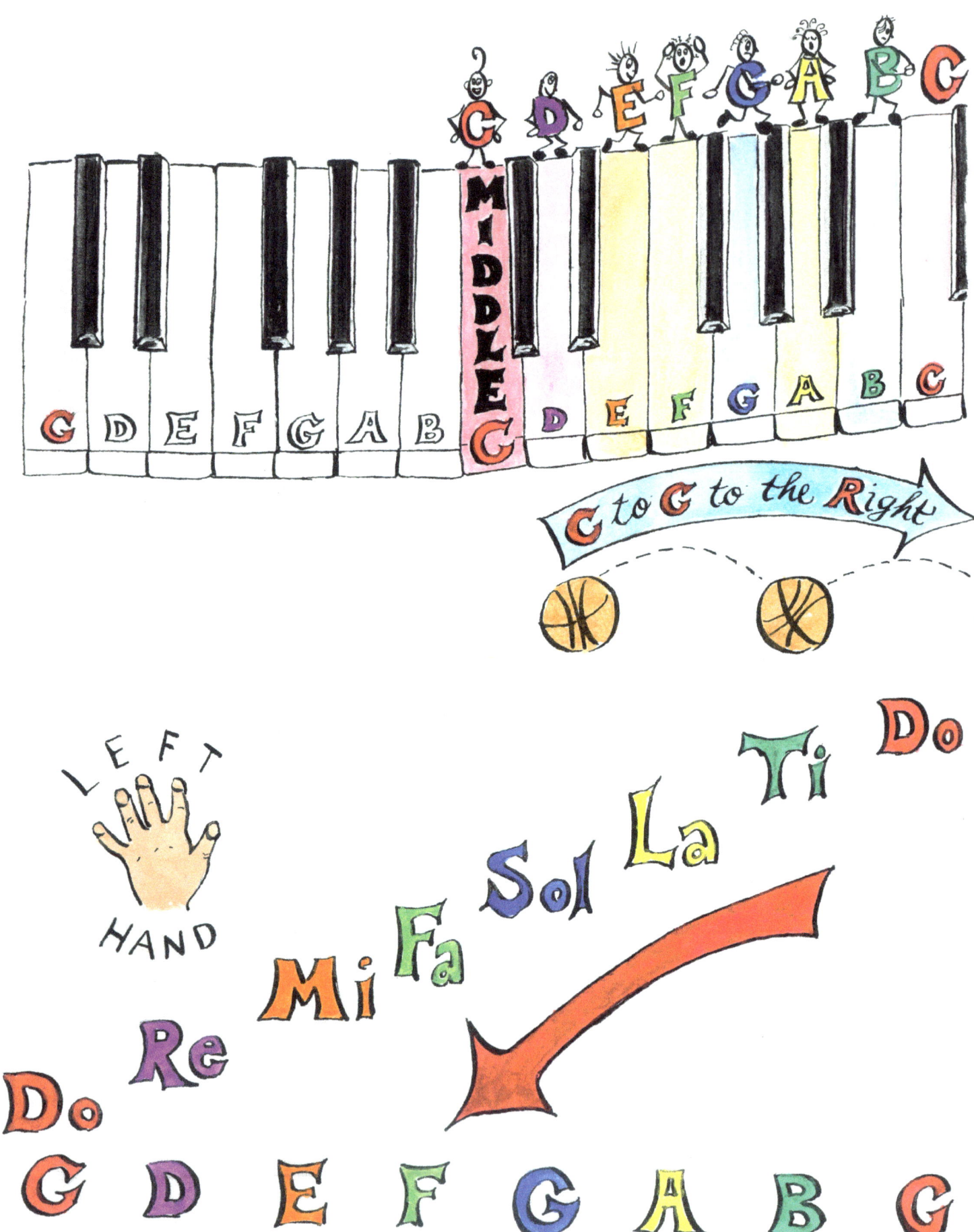

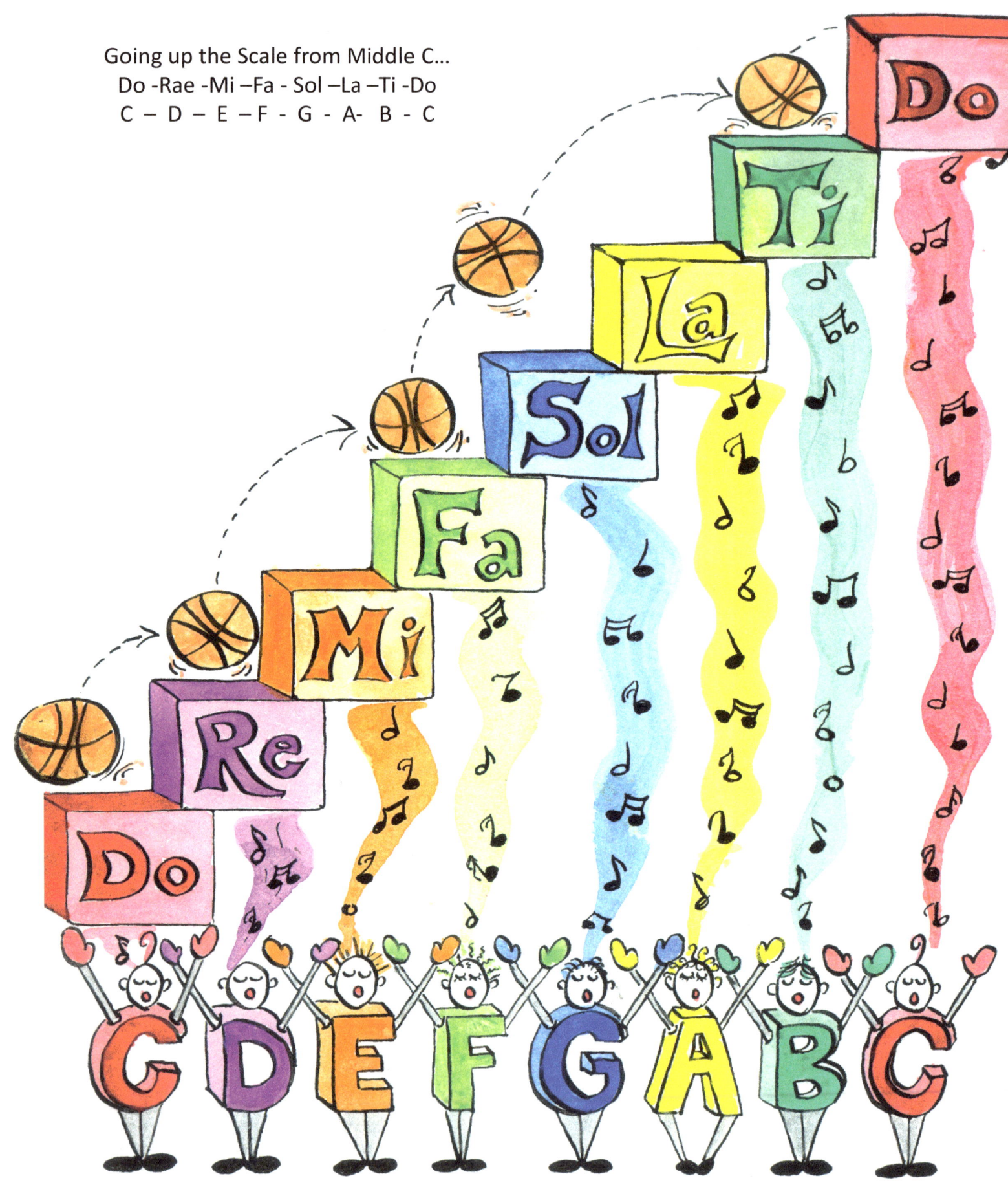

Then going down the Scale and back to Middle C ...
Do– Ti - La –Sol - Fa – Mi - Rae -Do
C – B – A – G – F – E - D - C

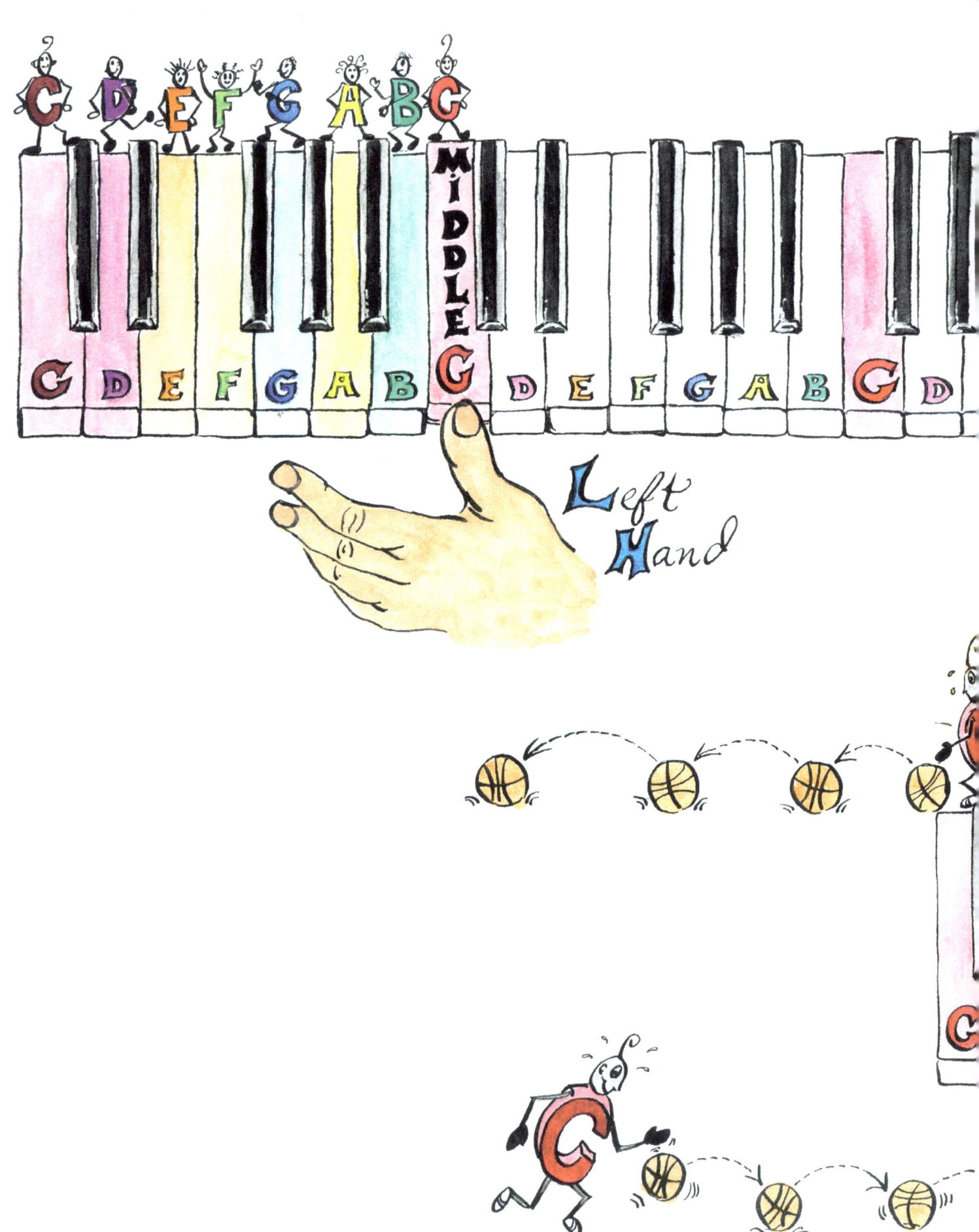

F G A B C

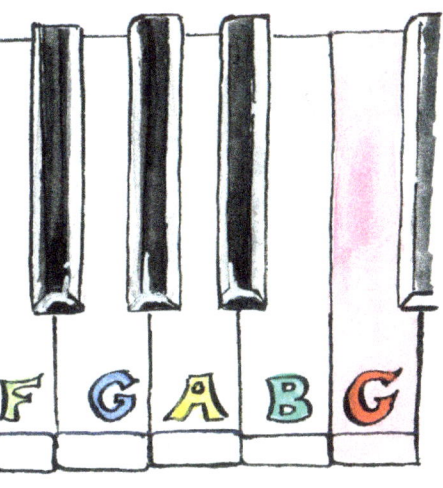

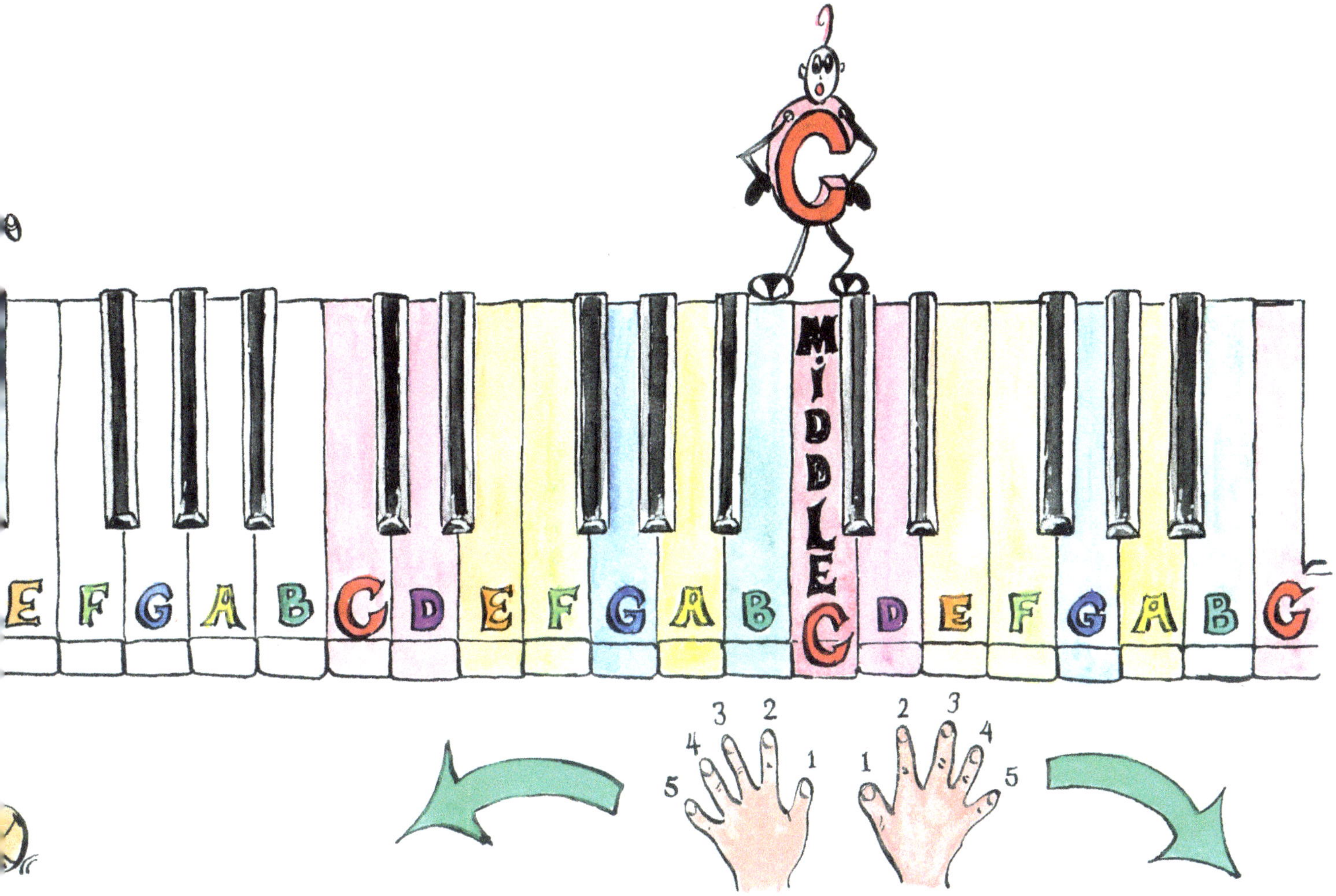
E F G A B C D E F G A B MIDDLE C D E F G A B C
5 4 3 2 1
1 2 3 4 5

Now, use your left thumb and down you'll be
Dribbling your left finger tips to the next lower C

Then, let your left fingers climb up again
And you'll arrive at Middle C therein

Flats

Each scale contains black and white keys
The white keys usually denote a note-up or down in degree,
While the black keys denote just a half-step up or down
Named sharps and flats for a half step up or half step down,

Just think of a staircase with shorter steps
For that's how steep a sharp or flat gets
It's a half step-up a sharp note makes
While a flat note a half-step down takes

Sharps

Each key signature reflects just what chords will resound
As each song is built on a chord's blending sounds
For, each song is written in a signature key
Noting apt chords, flats, sharps in proper degree

Children may struggle when learning to piano-play
Yet, reap enjoyment for the rest of their days

Though they may balk to practice day after day
Establishing a practice routine goes a 'long - long way'

Soon they'll realize how much they know
And want to continue and put on a show

For music is a universal language of sound
Providing positive sound media all around

The musical notes of the piano scales provide
A masterful way to improvise

To suit most voice ranges naturally
From soprano to alto to base
Allowing most to sing or dance in place

So, learn to read musical notes
Play the scales with high hopes

Embrace the piano for lifelong enjoyment
You may someday find musical employment

Dance if you like to any number of beats
For, it's always a delight to tap your feet

So, Begin at Middle C
And dream all you can be

For you may be a popular musician or singer by far
Maybe a classical pianist or famous-rock star

Write your own music, sing your own song
Life is more enchanting if shared with music along

Enjoy and listen to all musical scores
And life will open its magical sounding doors

Songs – Featuring Middle C

Words are only words without song
A song's beat and tone provide an audible 'strong'
Of what is trapped inside our very souls
As songs pour forth on emotional rolls
Letting our words vibrate in air
Songs give our voices – emotional flair!
To be shared and heard by all
Embracing us in a musical thrall!

And, as we sing aloud the words of a song
Mingling our hearts and souls, so strong!
We acknowledge all musical notes
Hummed or played as if by rote
As music carries the words and the way
For songs to be sung, our hearts to sway!

The home of songs emerges from piano keys
Notes played with chords, scales and synchronicity
Resounding from home base – Middle C
Residing in the midst of the piano keys,
Sung and played with vibrating intensity
Songs are the human voice of the piano keys!

Let's create more music and tunes
So songs and music ever bloom
Mingling evermore through space
With **Middle C**, their starting place!!

Then going down the Scale and back to Middle C ...
Do – Ti - La – Sol - Fa – Mi - Rae - Do
C – B – A – G – F – E - D - C

www.ingramcontent.com/pod-product-compliance
Lightning Source LLC
Chambersburg PA
CBHW060937180426
43194CB00049B/2974